ROBOT DREAMS

Paintings by Kriev

Kriev employs a bold color palette reminiscent of fauvism and Expressionism. Direct descendant of the Hlebine School, he promotes the emancipation from classical proportions in favor of über-subjective perception. Adept of the Art Brut and lowbrow movements, Kriev finds his artistic inspiration in popular culture, from the esoteric symbolism of the Mayans to Tim Burton's fantasy work. Cartoon surrealism infuses the paintings of this very imaginative artist.

After various exhibitions in Europe, Kriev settled in New England. Recently, he participated in the group exhibition "Visions of the Uncanny" alongside Sci-Fi illustrator Vincent Di Fate and surrealist artist Daniel Venjean. He was also featured on the cover of Artscope magazine in the fall of 2015.

I0432455

robot-kriev.deviantart.com

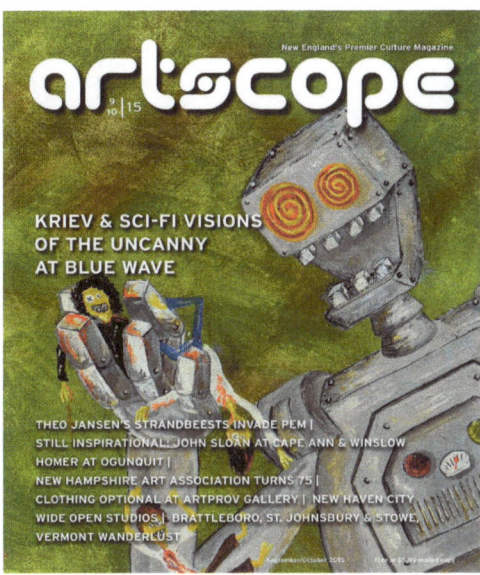

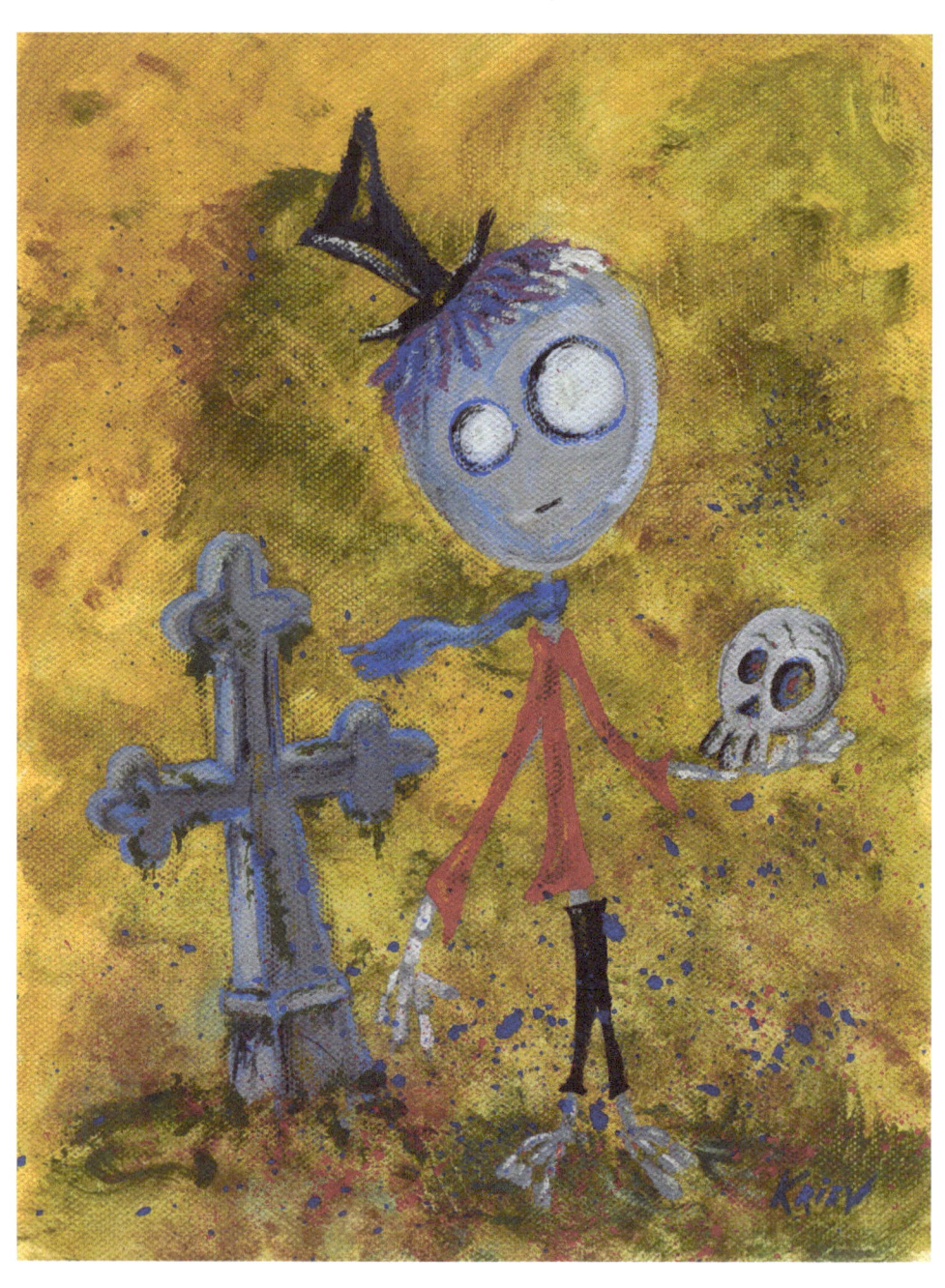

To Be or Not to Be

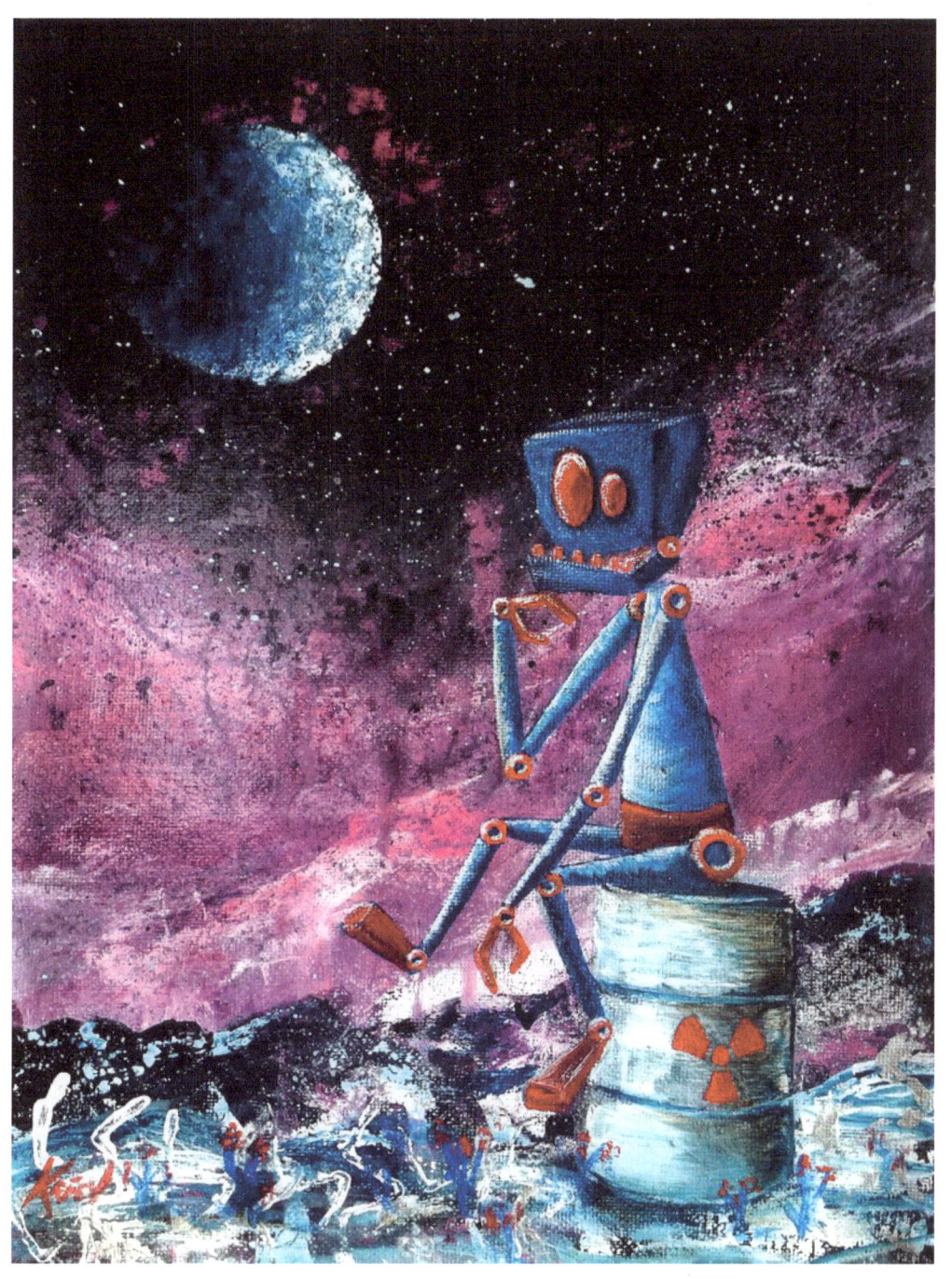

Think Robot

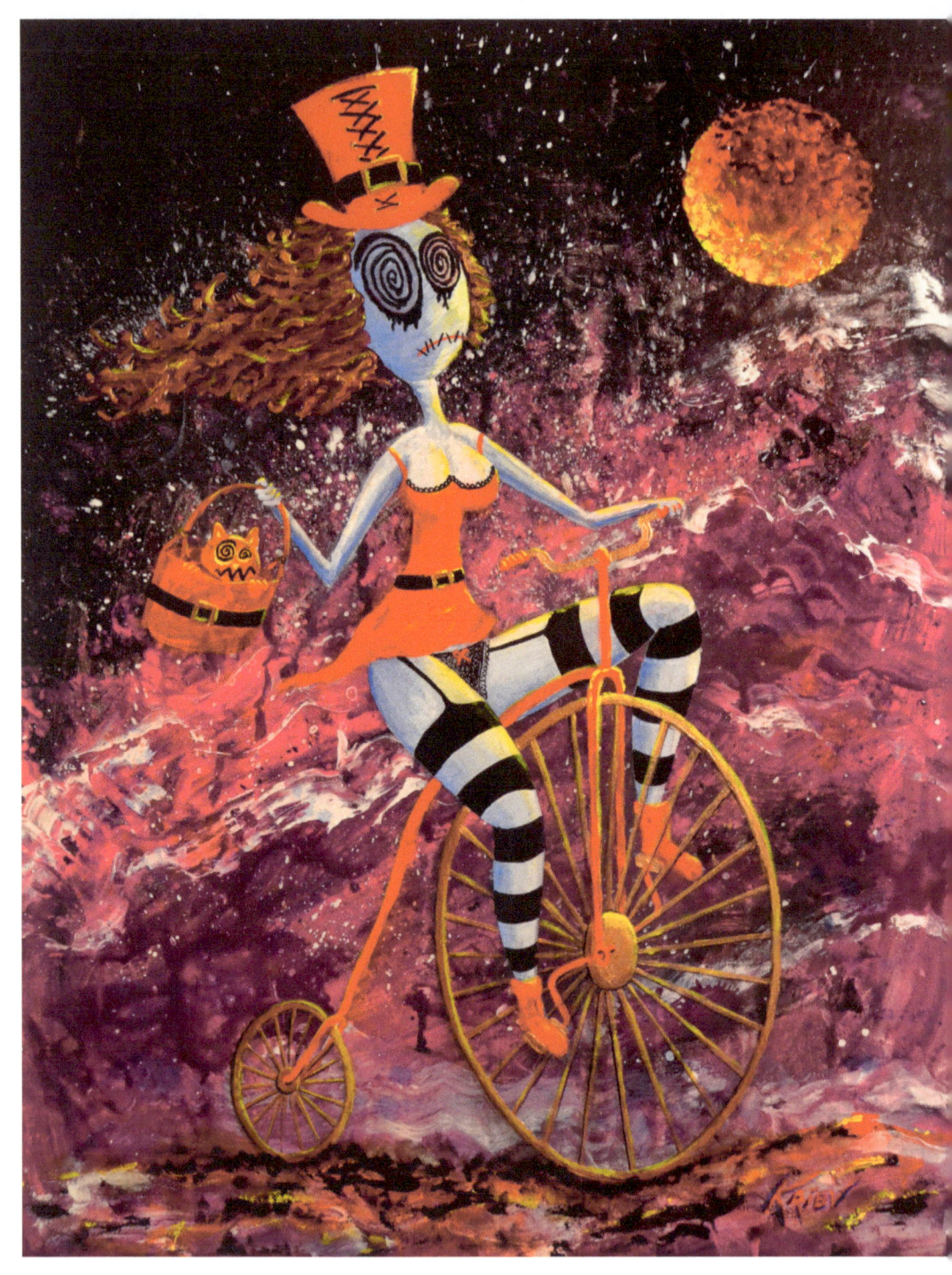

Red Hat

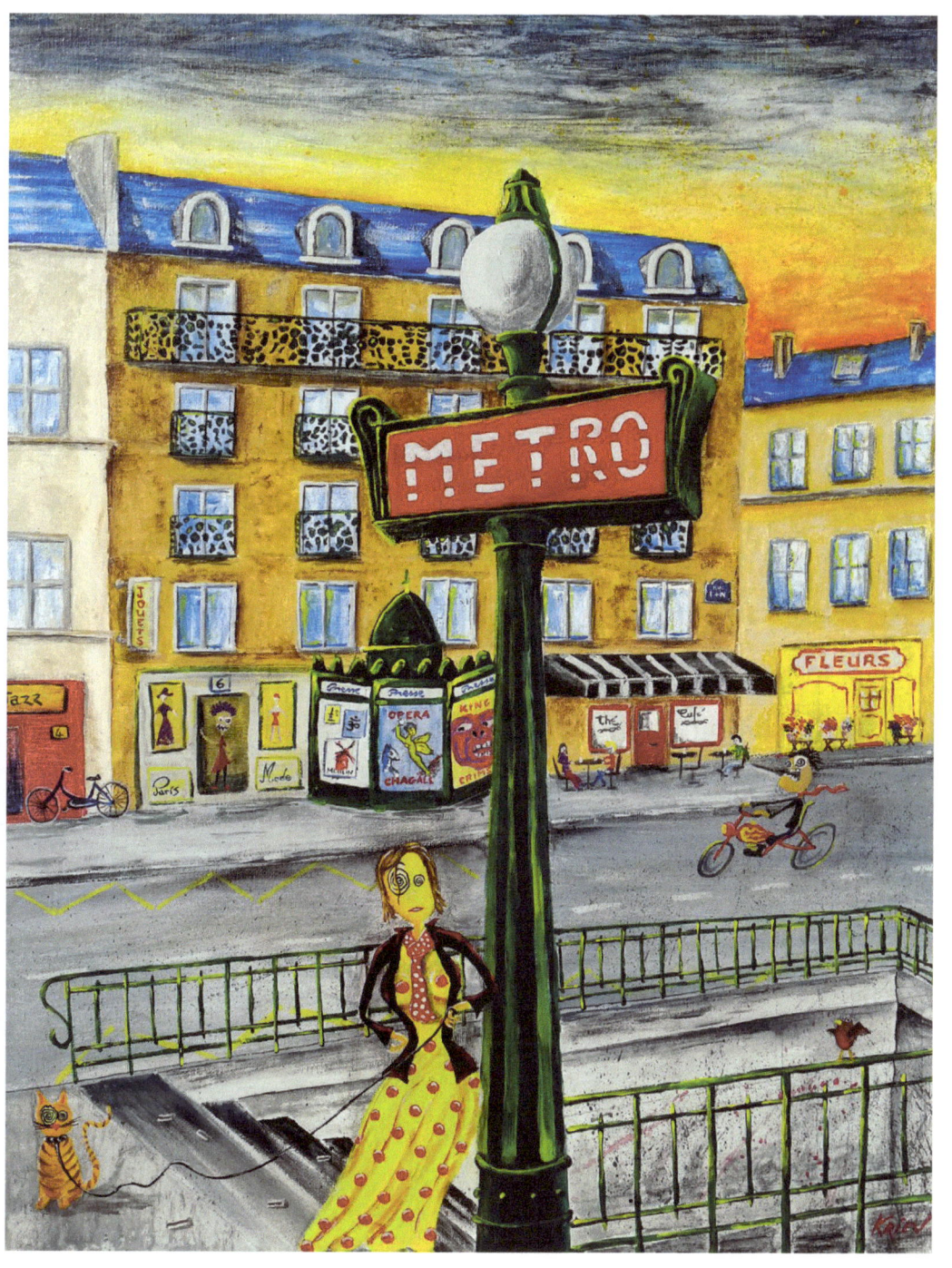

Metro

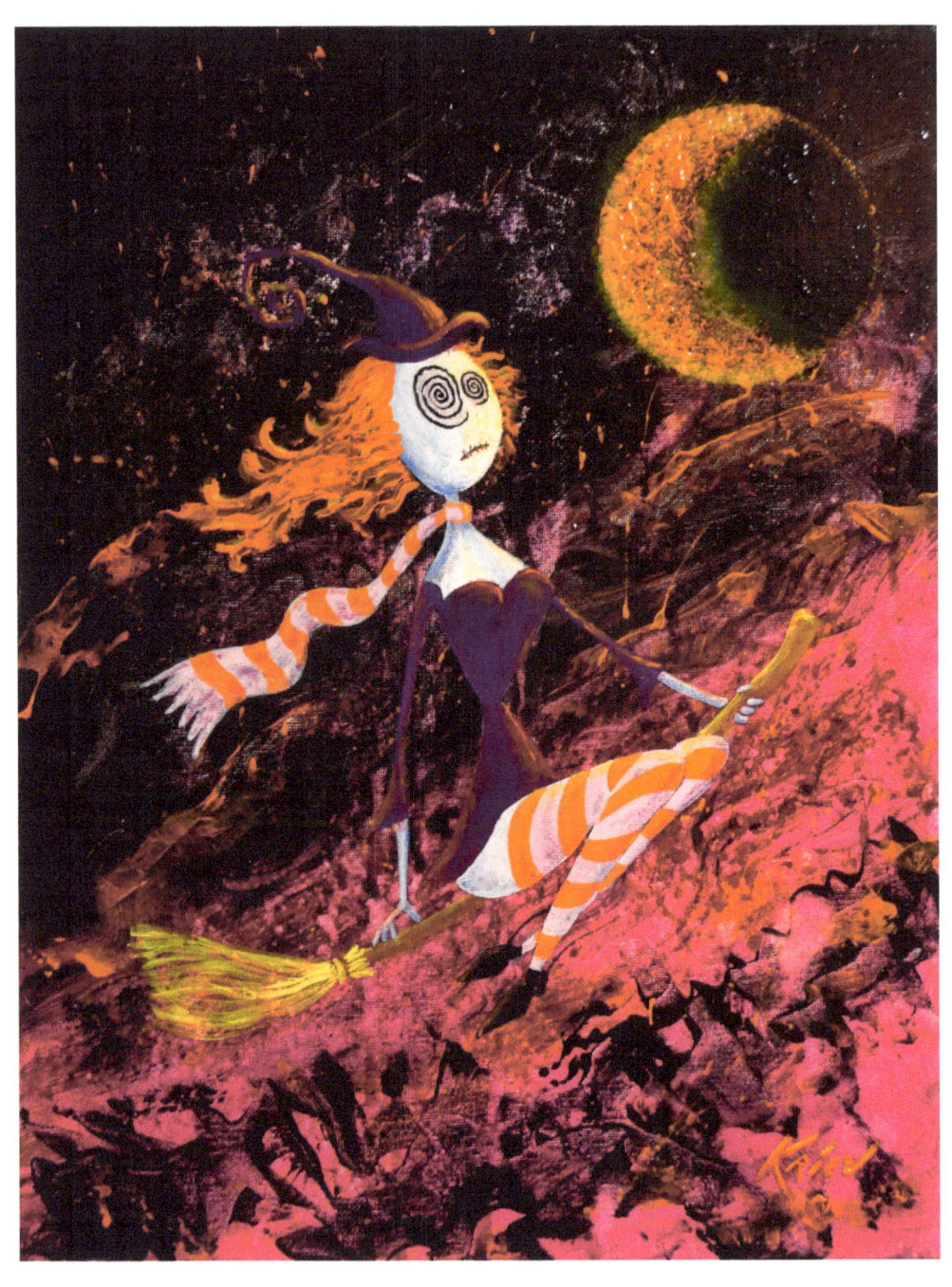

fire Witch

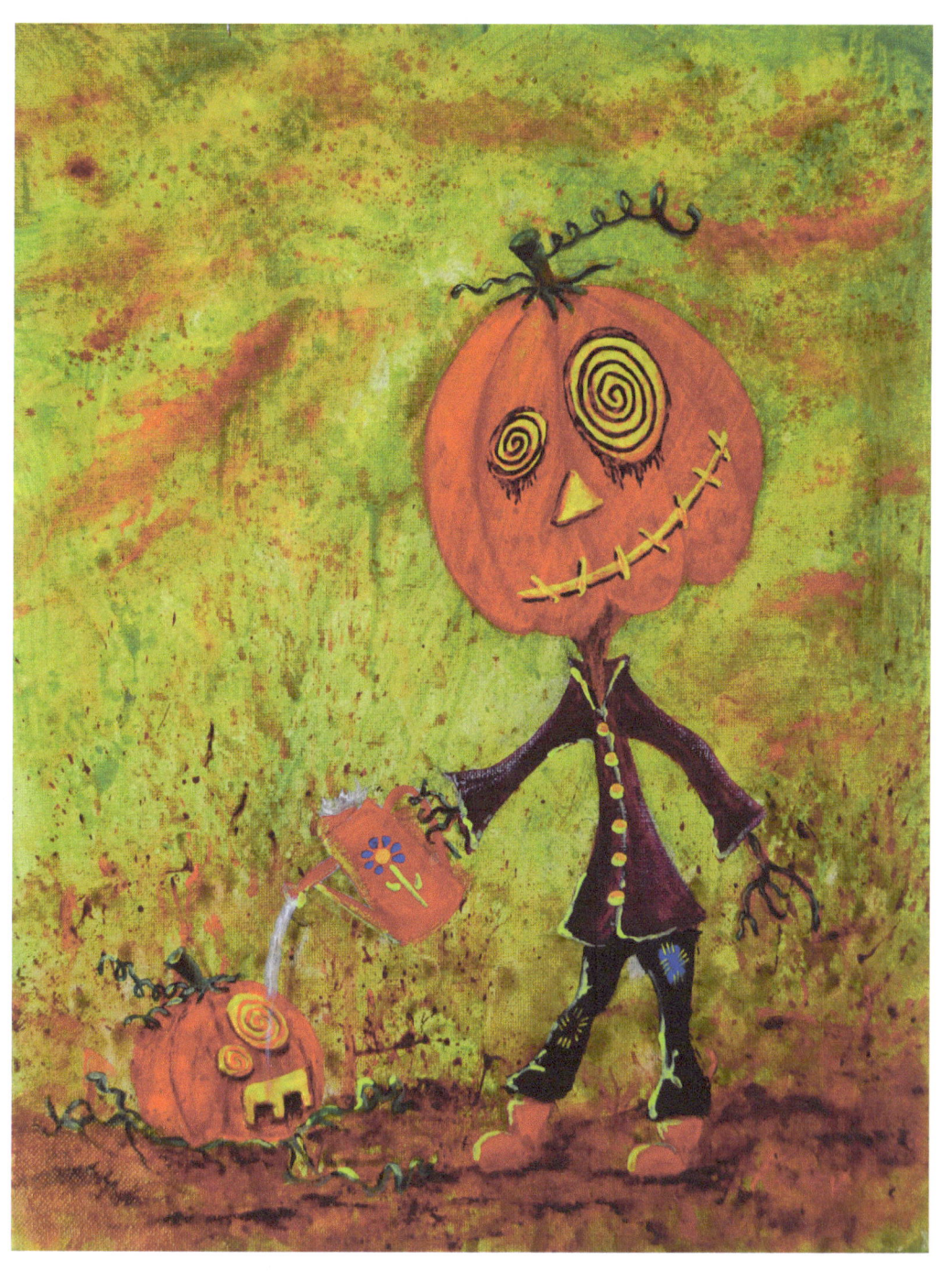

Country Pumpkins

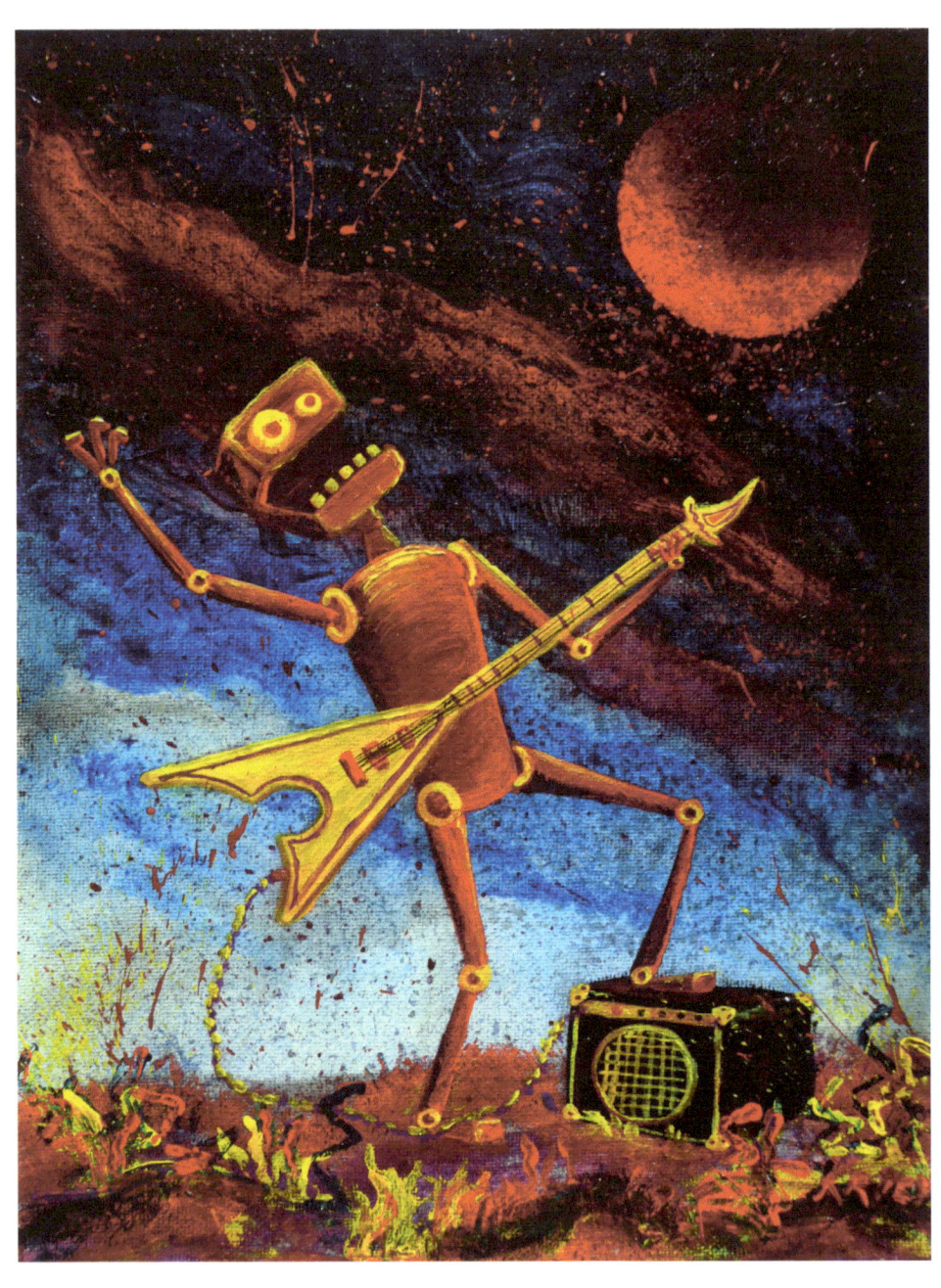

Red Rock

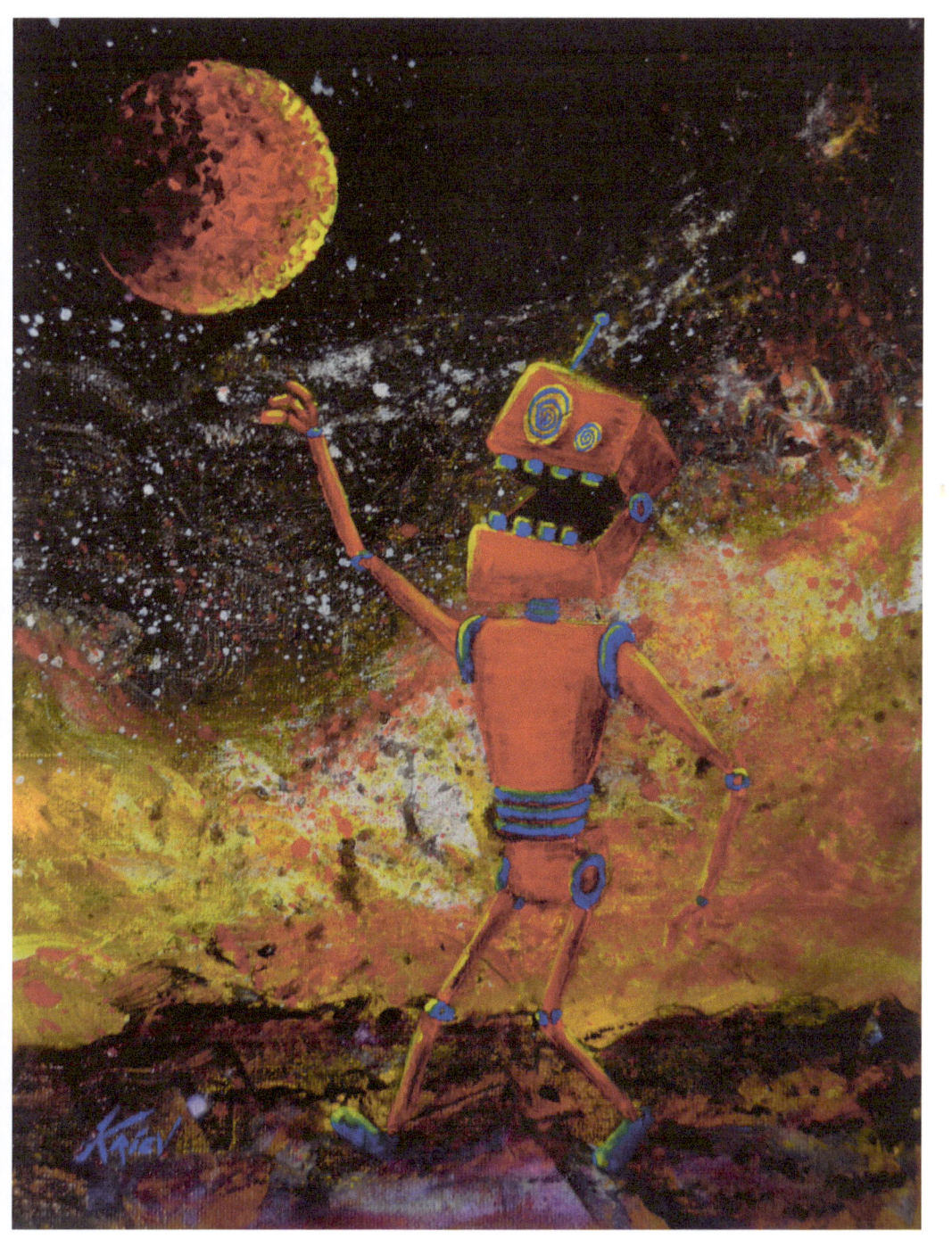

Fly Me to the Moon

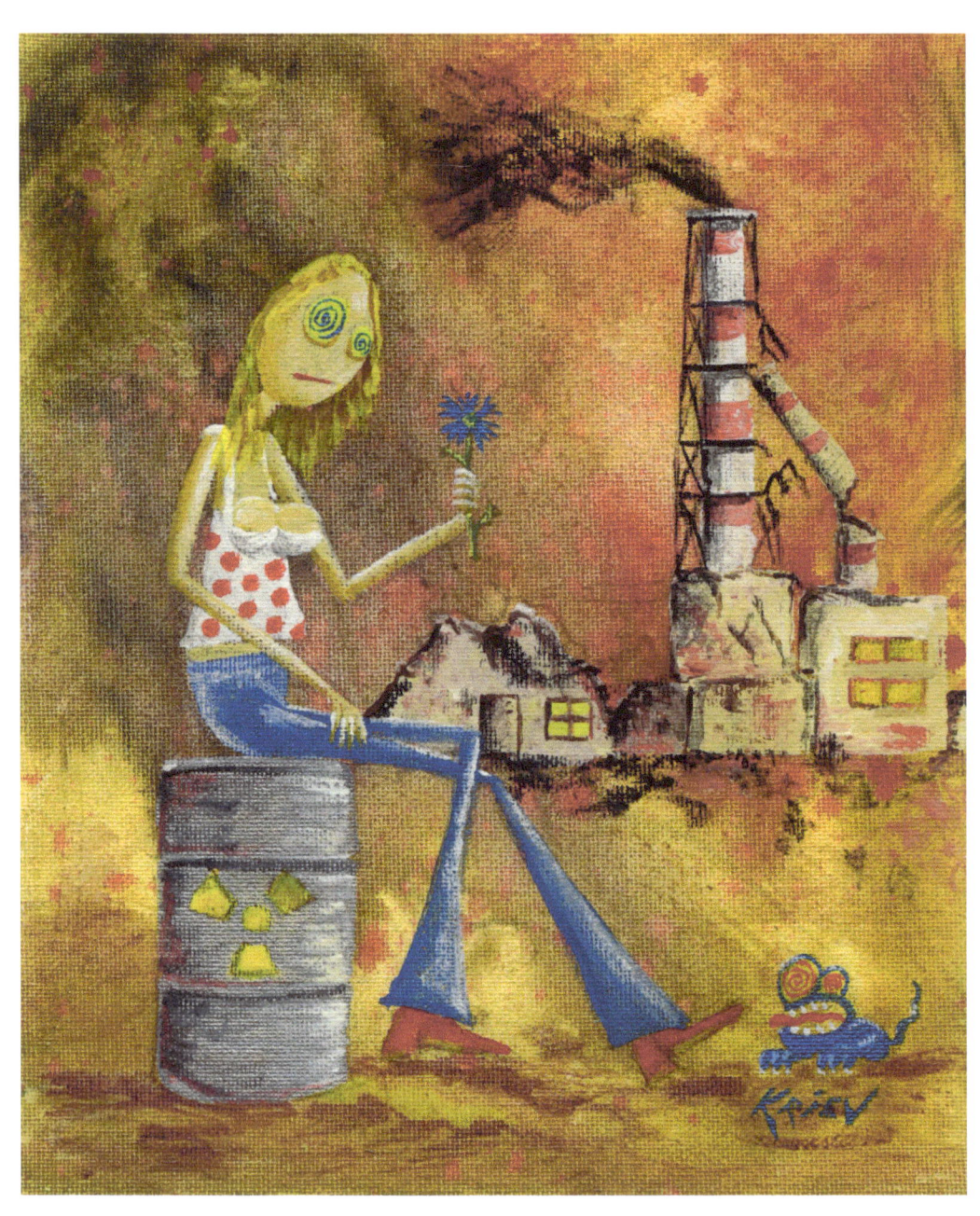

Vasilek

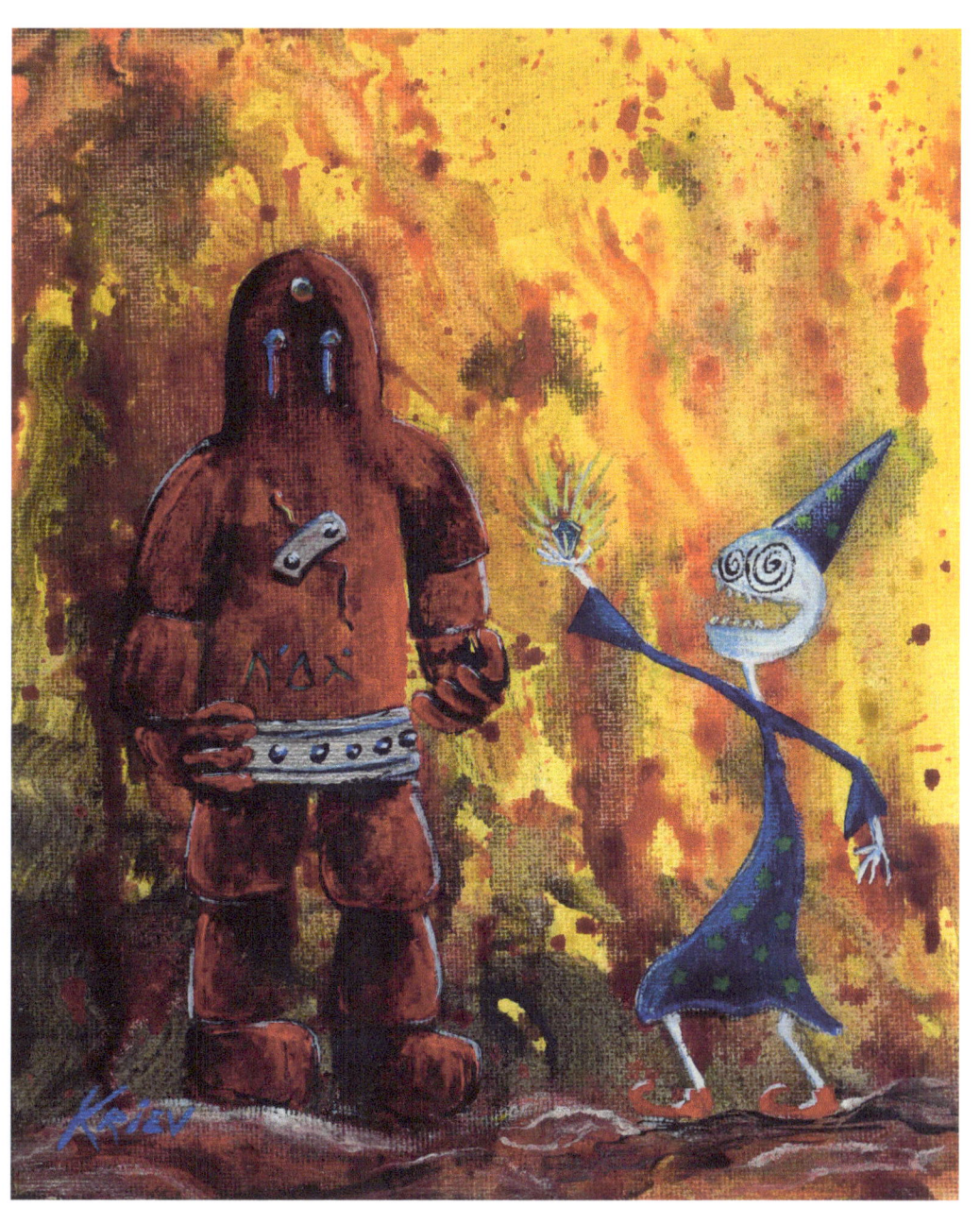

Golem

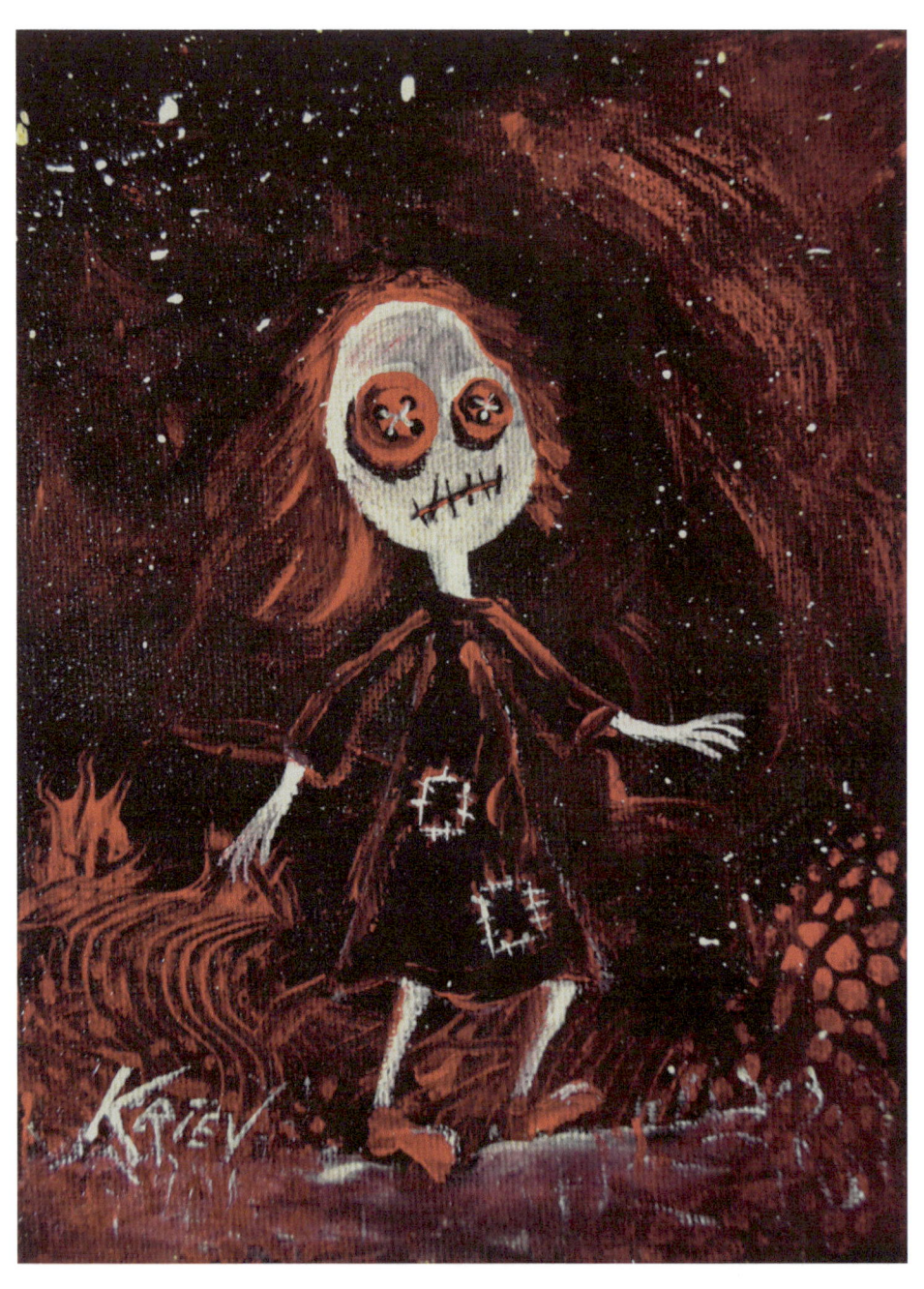

Cute as a Button

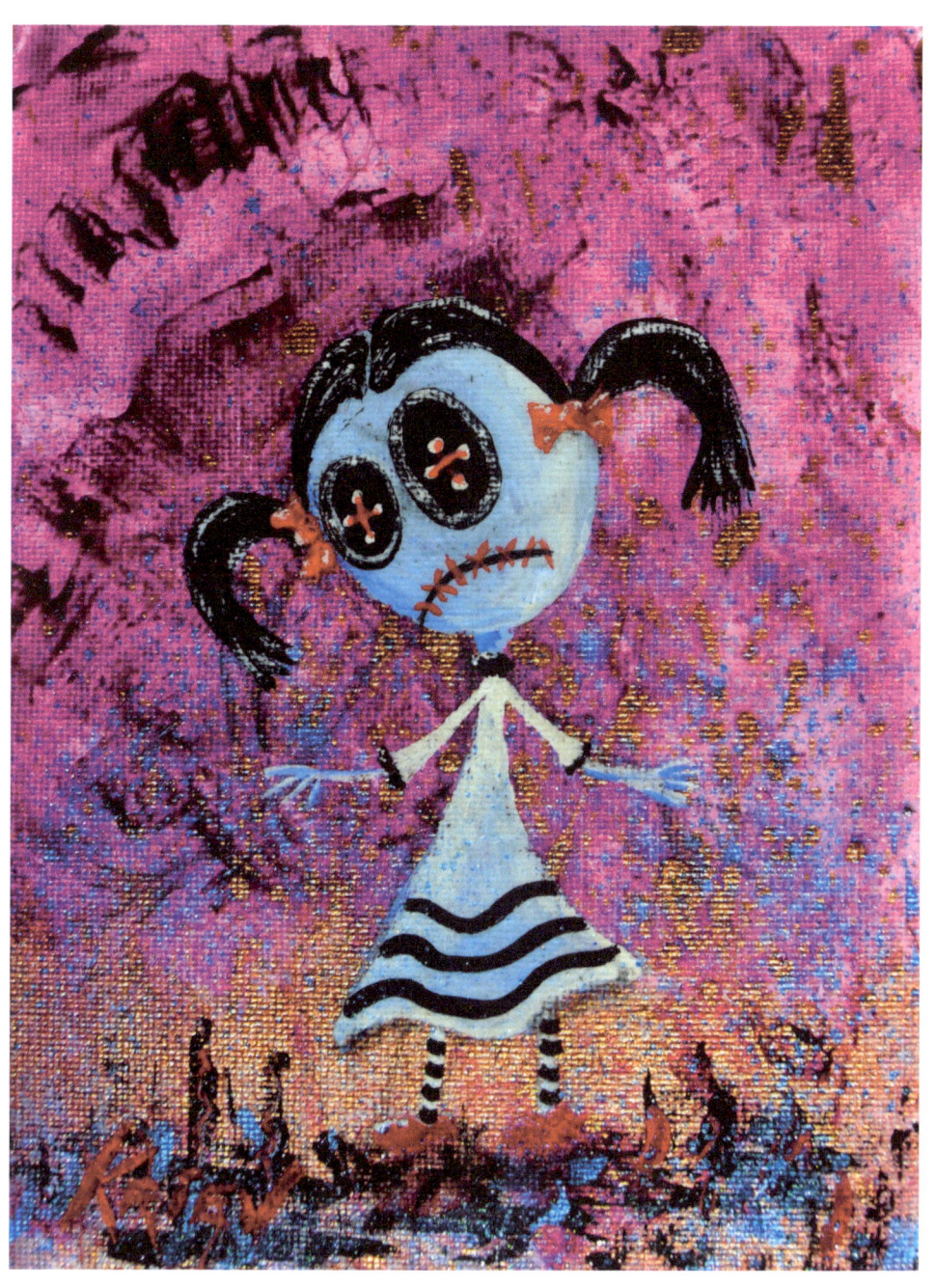

Gothic Cutie

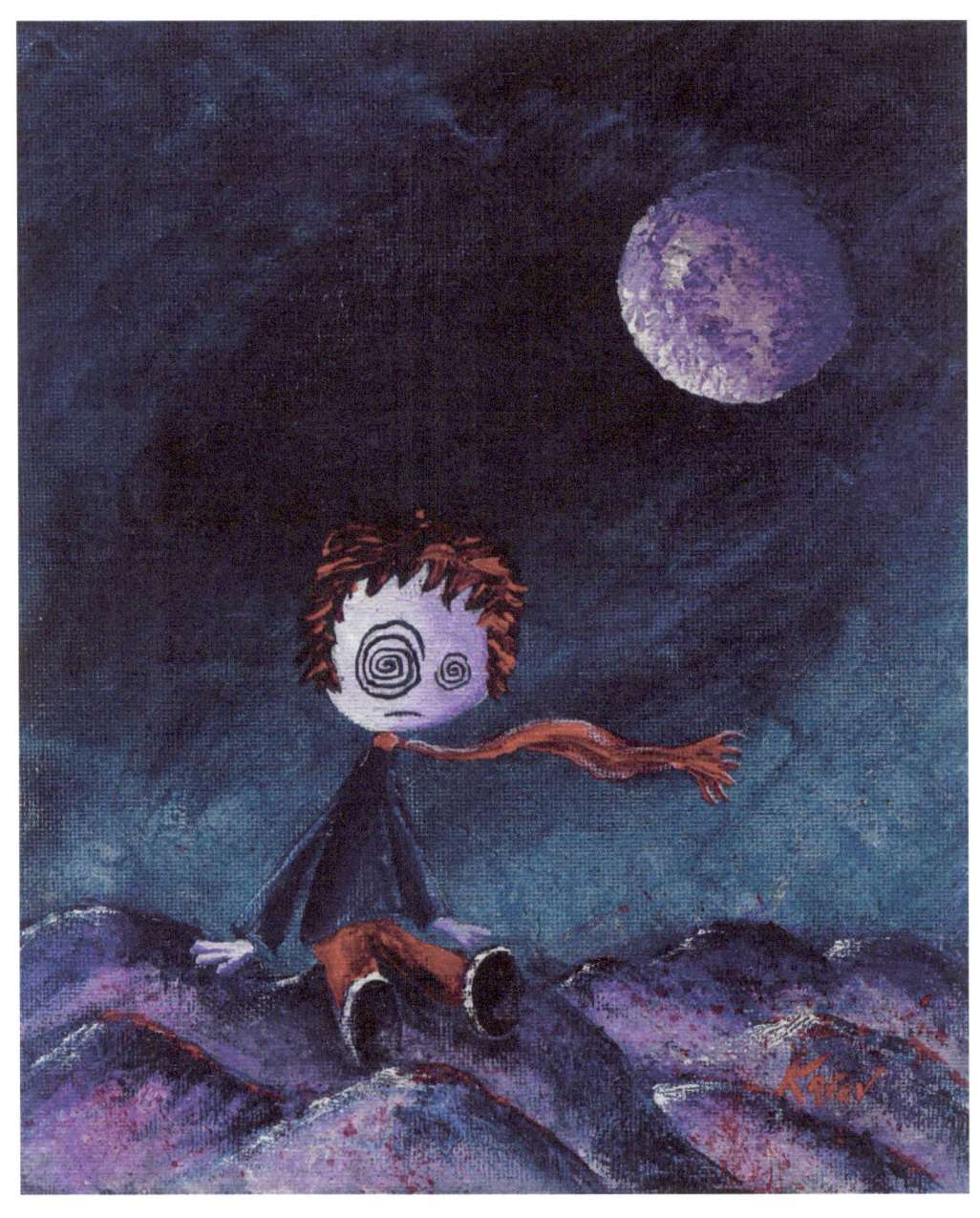

Under a Violet Moon

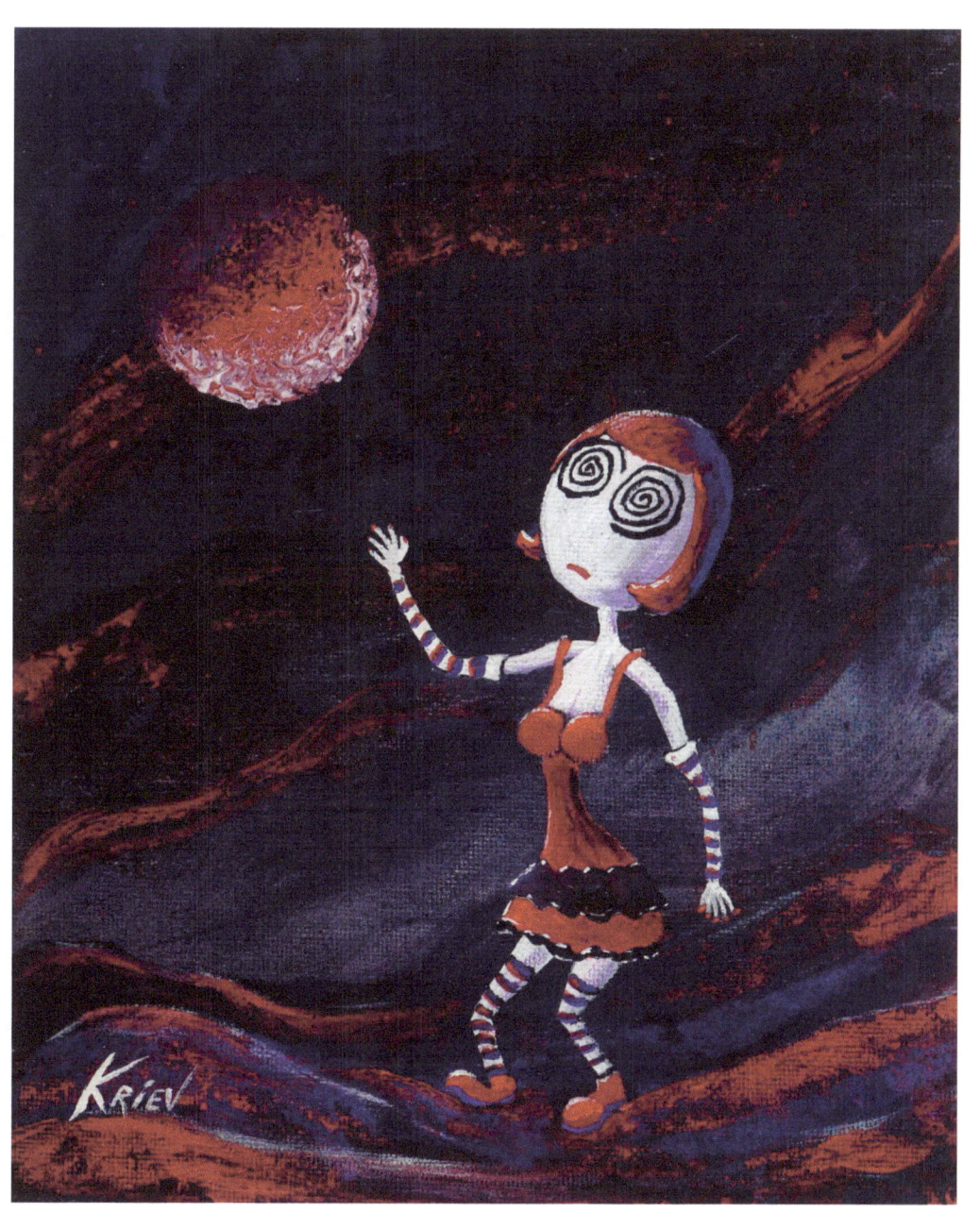

Red Planet

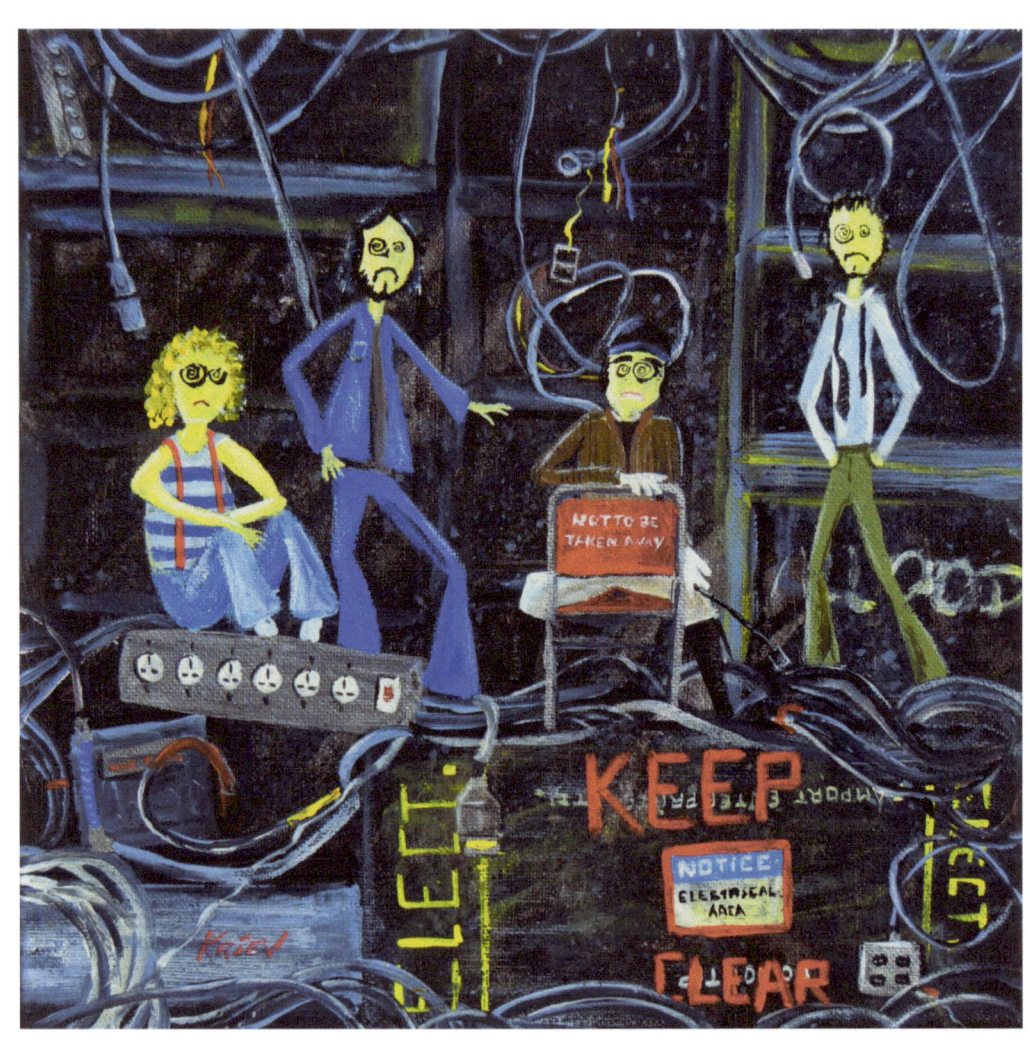

Who Are They

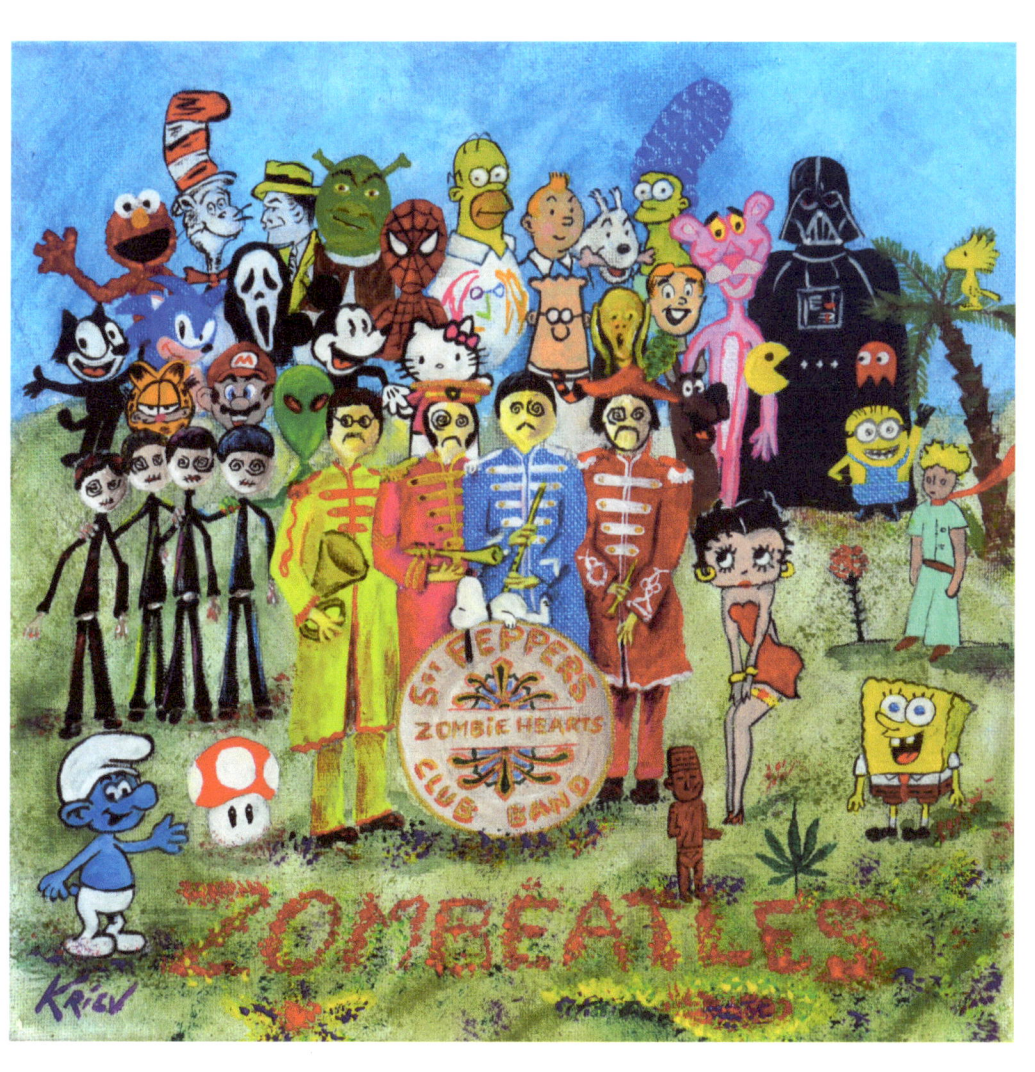

Zombie Hearts Club Band

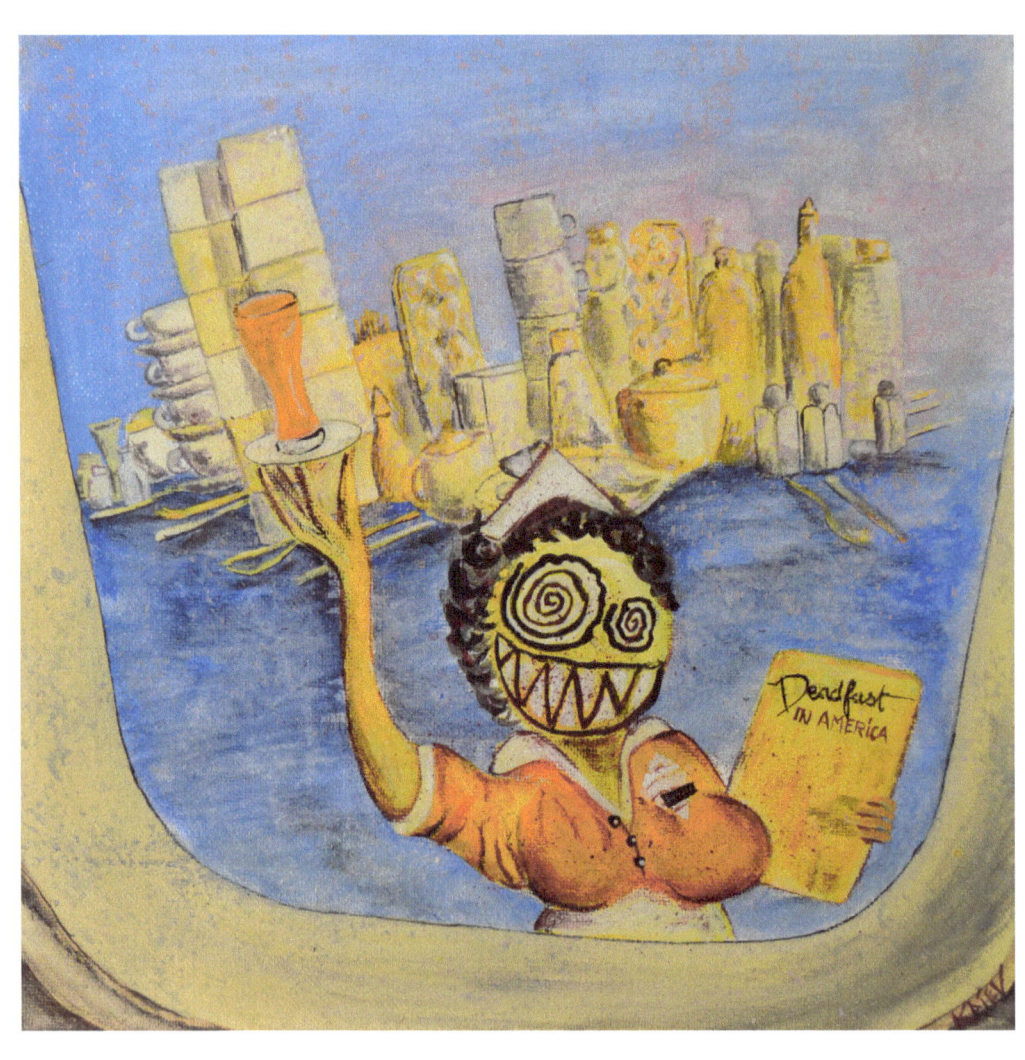

Deadfast in America

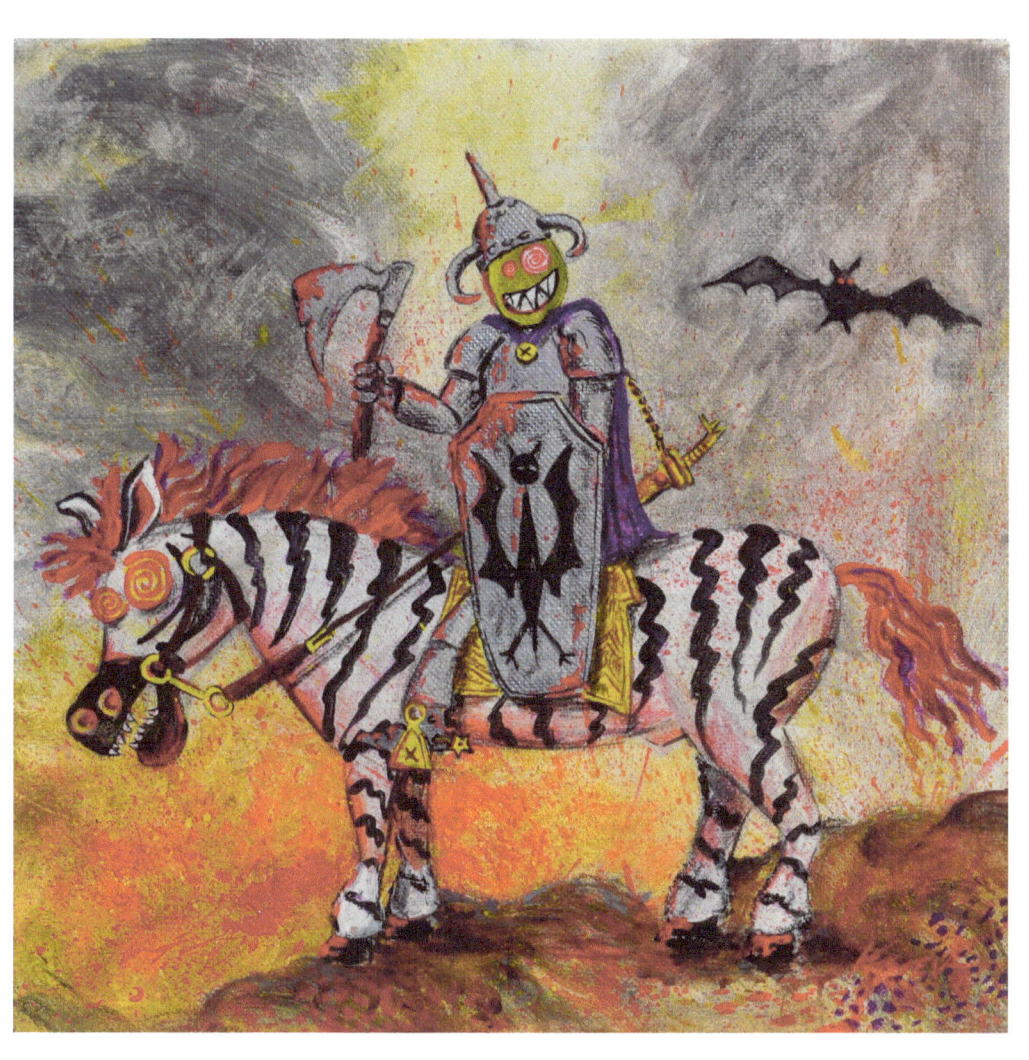

Zombie Hatchet

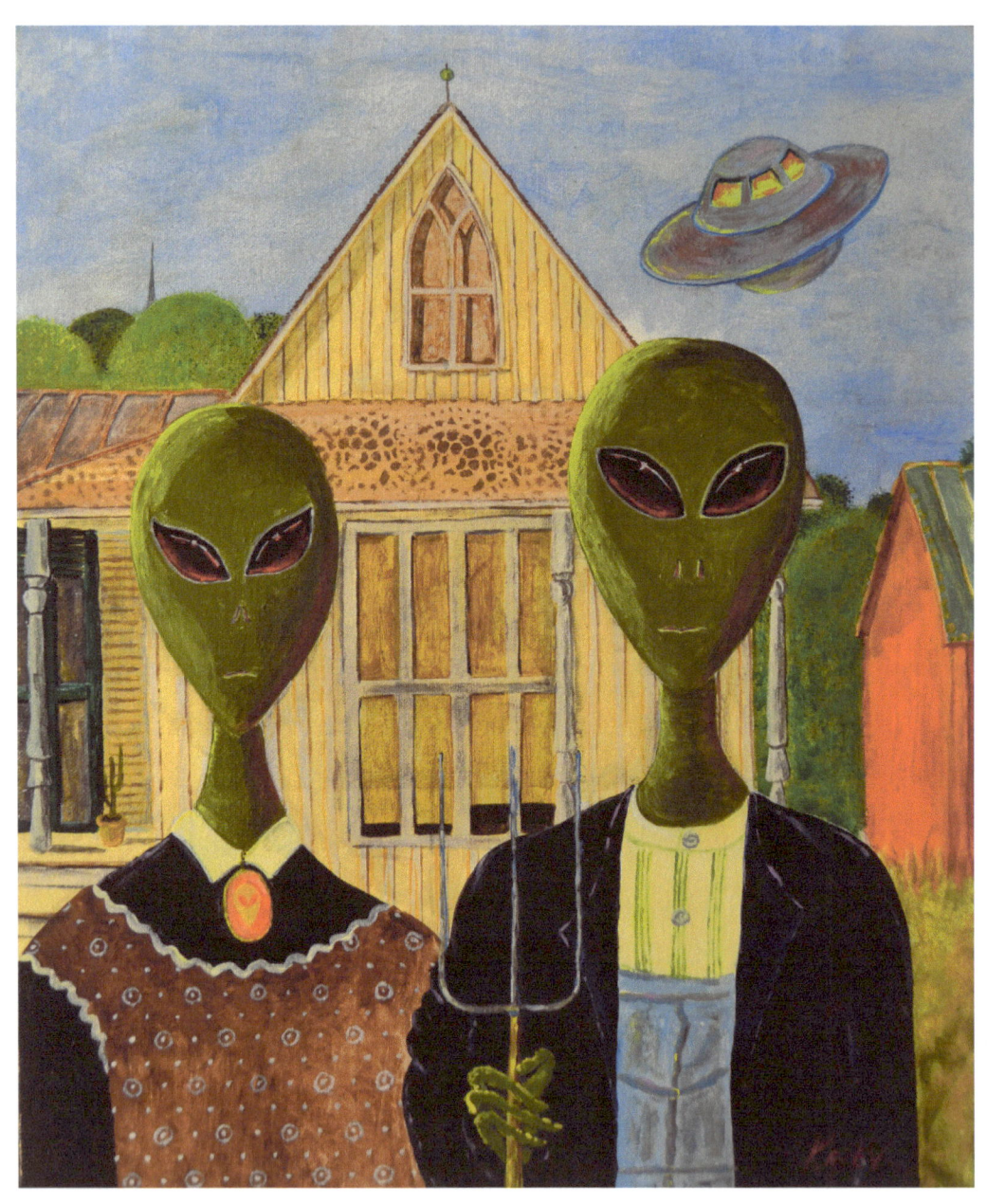

Alien Gothic

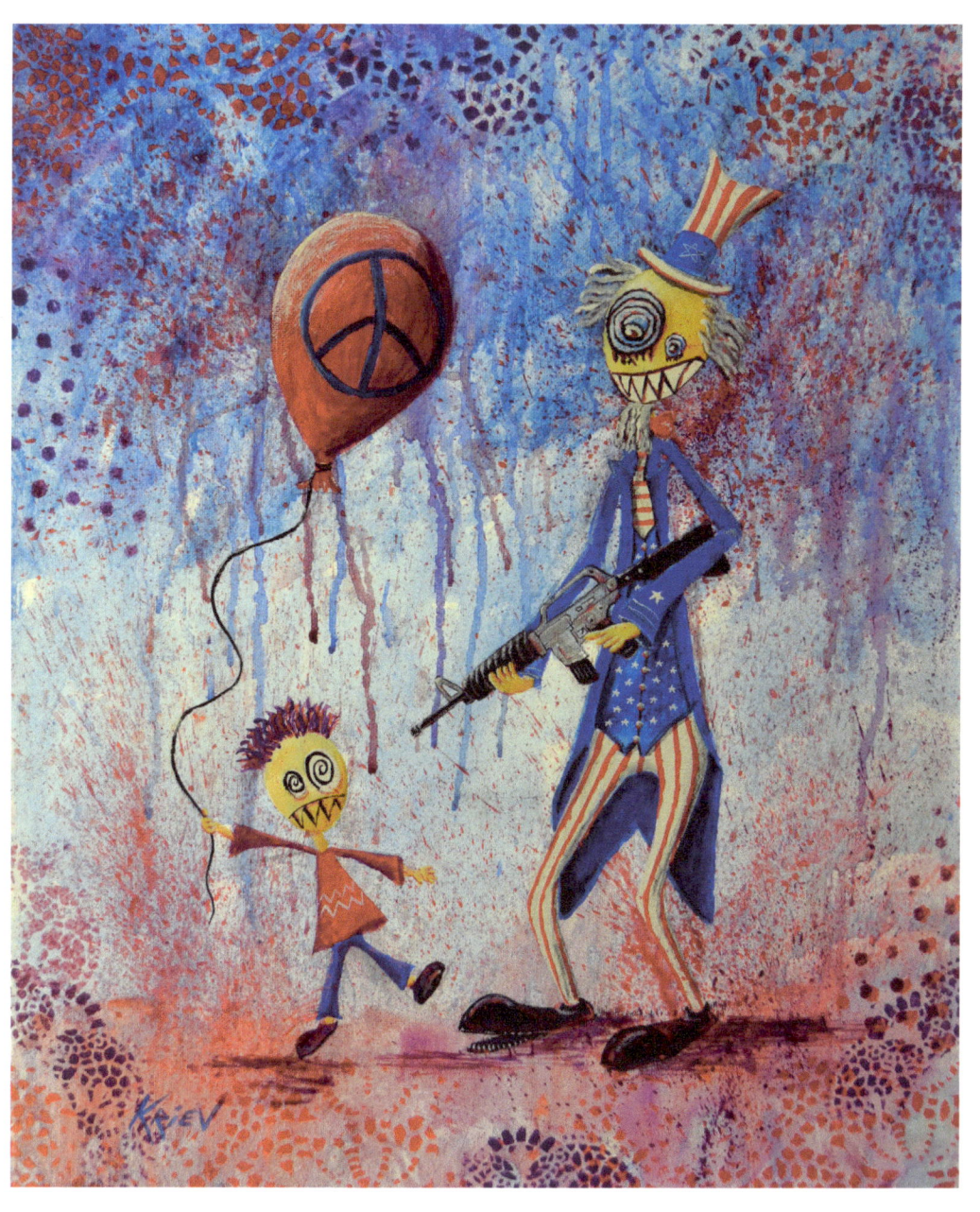

Independence Dead

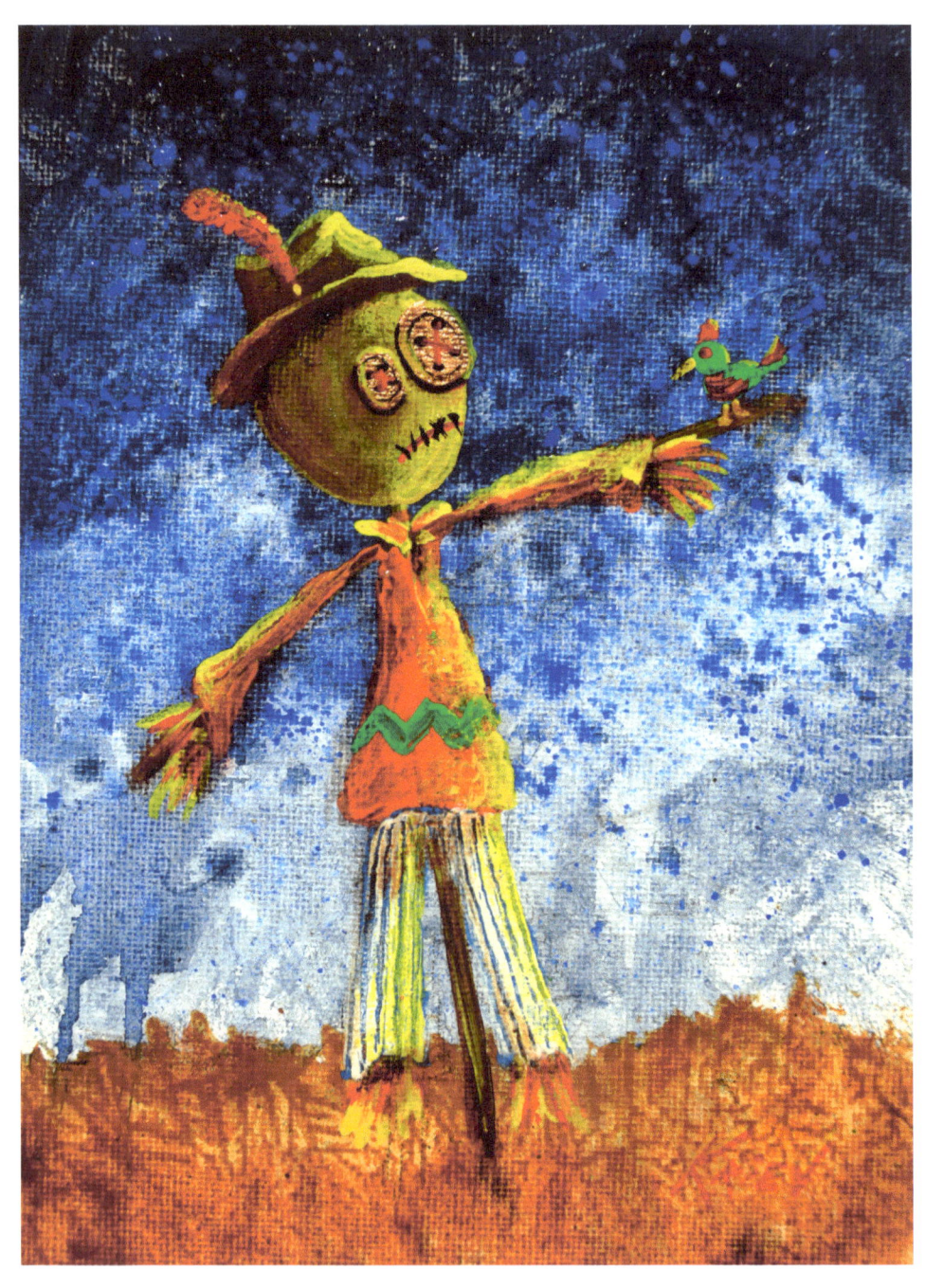

A Scarecrow

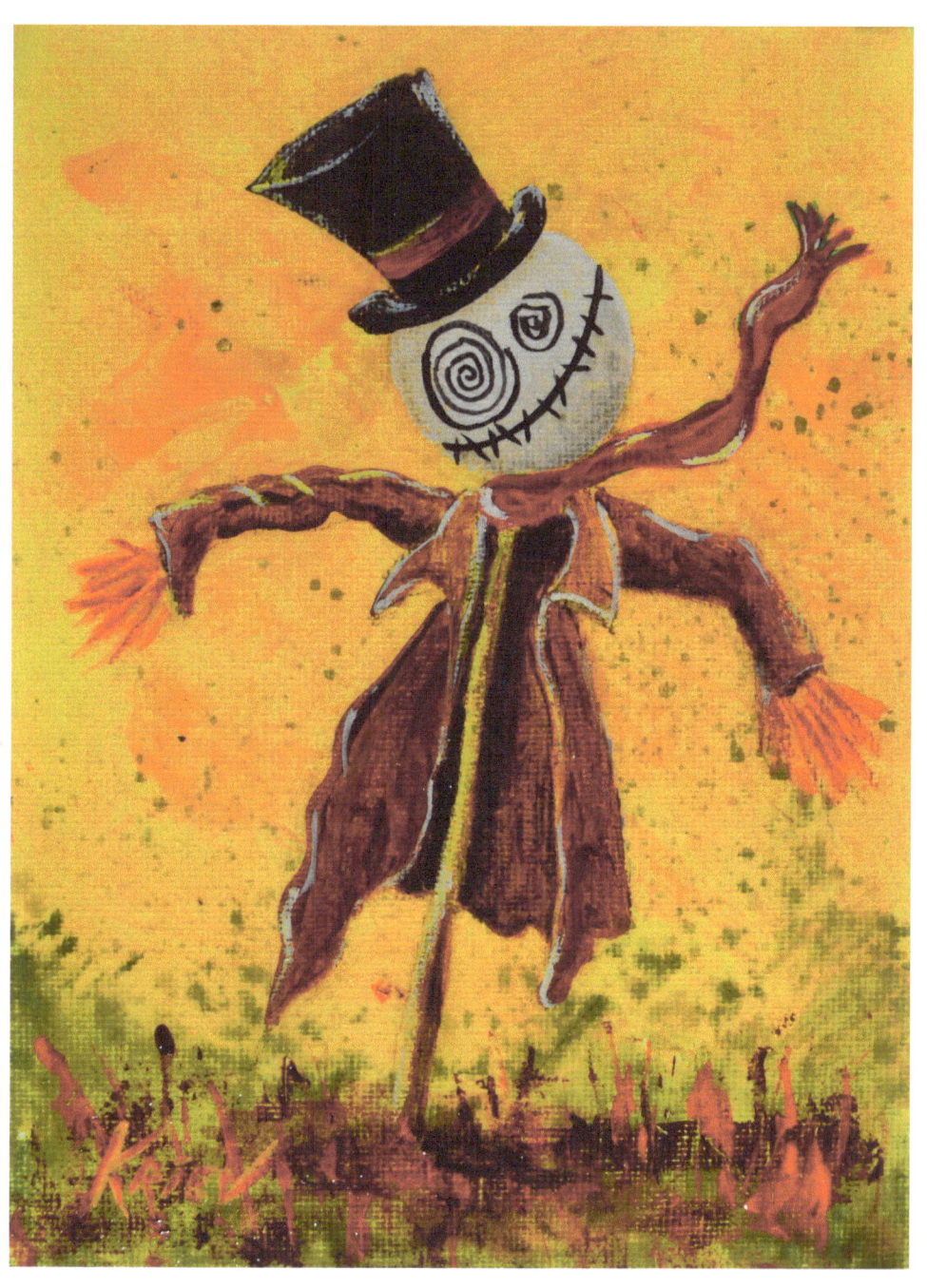

Another Scarecrow

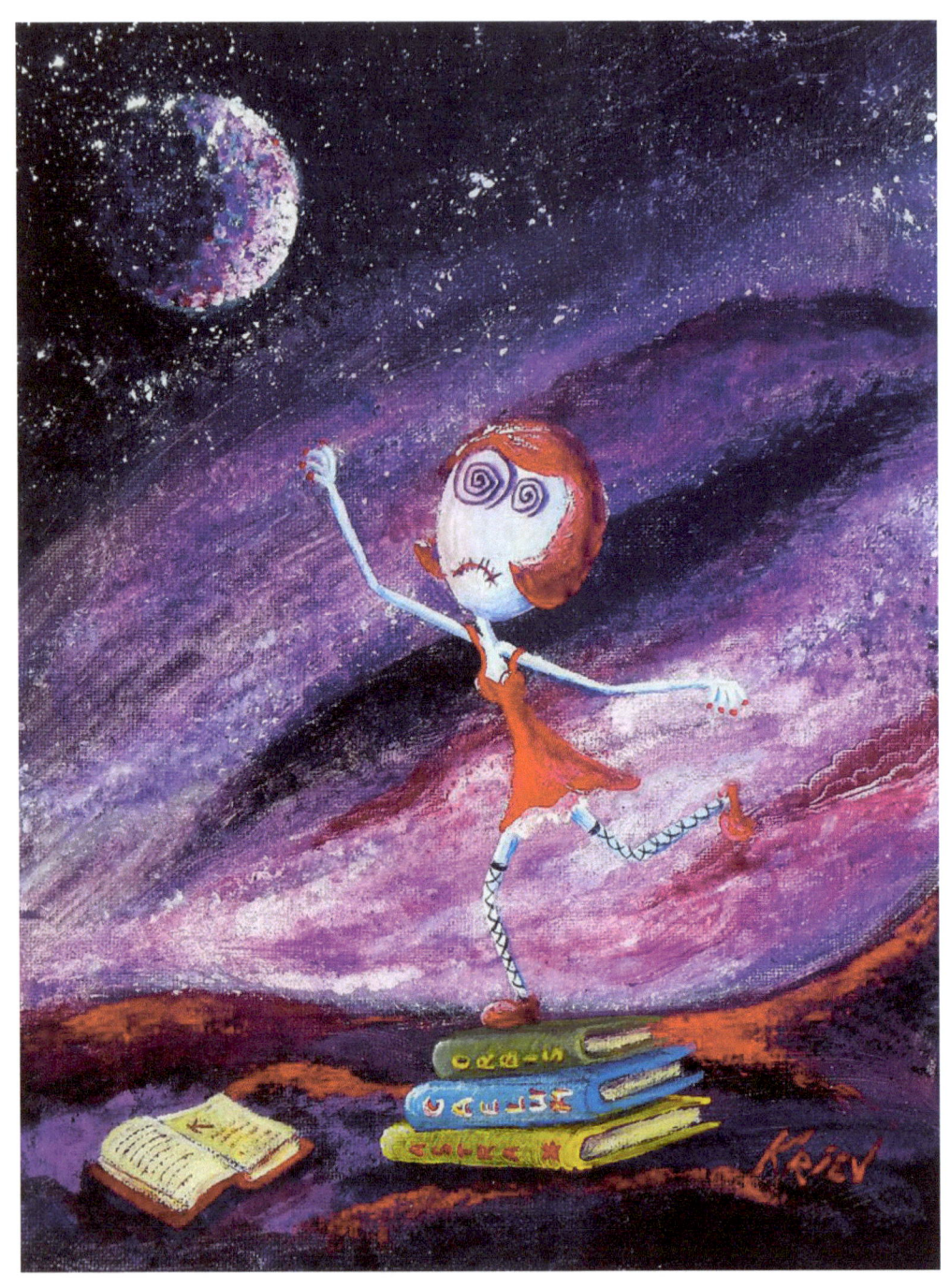

Ad Astra